Amazon Echo

The Ultimate Amazon Echo Beginner's User Guide to Make The Most Of Your Alexa (Echo, Alexa, Dot, 2019 manual, apps Book, Amazon Alexa, step-by-step user guide, user manual)

ANDREW HOWARD

CONTENTS

Introduction

Amazon continues to revolutionize the way we use technology with its suite of Amazon Echo devices. The Echo devices can easily be dubbed the smart phones of the home. Not only can these devices aid you in performing simple tasks, pulling up information and even making phone calls, they can also connect to the appliances and products that you use around your home every day. Echo products are more than just Bluetooth speakers. With Alexa, Amazon's digital assistant, at the heart of every device they get smarter with every update.

Amazon has even recently updated the physical features of some of its devices. This included updating the microphone pattern of the Echo Dot to enhance its audio capabilities, adding a larger display to the Echo Show as well as adding a temperature sensor to the Echo Plus.

Though the first Echo was originally released in 2015, Amazon continues to enhance not just it's physical functions but Alexa as well. At CES 2019, a convention hosted by the Consumer Technology Association for consumer technology, Alexa continued to wow the masses with its possibilities. Although Alexa can still handle the basics it has been added to everything from multi cookers to smart glasses.

Echo and Alexa have continued their budding partnership to bring its users more than just the standard Echo speaker. Other Echo options include the Echo Spot, the Echo Dot, the

Echo Show and even the Echo Dot Kids. This is far from the entirety of the list, as the Echo offerings continue to grow each day.

This guide will give you insight on what Alexa can do for you and even provide step by step instruction on how to activate a variety of functions. It will also provide information on how to setup the various variations of your Echo device.

Chapter 1: Setting Up Your Device for Use & Getting Started with Alexa

Setting up your Amazon Echo device is quick and easy no matter what device you have. This chapter will walk you through the setup of not just the standard Amazon Echo but of the Echo Dot, Echo Show, Echo Spot and the Echo Tap as well. This chapter will also aid you in preparing Alexa for use.

Note: If your Echo device was purchased via Amazon it will come associated to the Amazon account under which it was purchased unless otherwise specified at the time of purchase.

What's in the Box?

Don't expect any bells and whistles in your Amazon Echo device's packaging. There are few items which come standard in the Echo boxes. They generally include the Echo device; a short user quick start guide and the AC cord and adapter. These items and your smartphone are all you need to begin setup on your new device.

However, if you are using the Amazon Tap you will have slightly different items in your box. The Tap, although no longer on sale via Amazon's website, comes with the following items:
- Amazon Tap Device
- Charging Cradle

- MicroUSB cable & adapter
- Quick Start Guide

Before beginning setup of any one of the Echo devices, make sure that you have installed and logged into the Amazon Alexa companion application. The application is available on a variety of platforms, including the following:

- IOS (iPhone)
- Fire OS (Amazon Devices)
- Android
- Alexa.Amazon.com (browser)

Users have the option to use their Desktop browser from Amazon's Alexa site. For anyone opting to use a Fire Tablet, the Alexa application should come preinstalled on your device. After you have downloaded the corresponding application to your smart phone, you are ready to unbox and set up your device.

Setting Up Your Echo Device

The setting process of the Echo is simple. First, you should place it onto a secure surface ready for setup or anywhere within reach of a power outlet.

The rubber base of the Echo keeps it secure and prevents it from marking surfaces. Its power input is located under the base. You can see a small hole on the edge of the base. It enables the adaptor cable to reach the input whilst keeping the Echo upright. Then you can see above this hole a small white LED, it indicates when the Echo is receiving power.
Once you have plugged in your Echo, a ring of blue LEDs on top of the Echo will light up and rotate. Then in about one minute, the blue light will change to orange. Then Alexa will greet you and prompt you to follow the setup instructions via the Echo/Alexa app. If the Echo doesn't light up, you should check your power outlet and ensure that the AC adaptor is connected to the Echo correctly.

Once you have successfully placed and plugged in your device you are ready to setup your Echo using your smartphone. If you have not done so, sign into the Amazon account you desire to use with your device. This will enable you to connect to the internet, any third-party applications you wish to use and ultimately utilize your device.

If you already have an Alexa device actively using your same Amazon account and Wi-Fi connection and you have purchased one of the following devices: second-generation or newer Echo Plus, Echo Show or third-generation Echo Dot. The device will attempt to connect to your Wi-Fi using Amazon's new Simple Setup. If simple setup fails, proceed as described below.

Once you have logged into your Alexa account, select the navigation icon located on the top left corner. From there select "Add Device" and choose the type of device you are looking to connect.

Another way to navigate to your devices menu is to select "Devices" along the bottom tray of the application. Here you will see already paired devices or groups you have created. To add your new device, you will select the plus sign on the upper right hand corner. When prompted, select "Add Device".

You will then need to follow the on-screen prompts to finish adding the device to your account. These prompts include the type of device, Echo Device, headphones, lights etc., as well as the specific device, Echo Dot, Tap, show, etc. In this case, you will choose the first option of "Echo". The app will then direct you on how to setup the Wi-Fi on your device, this should be completed when the light on your device has turned orange after plugging it in.

If you do not see the orange light, press and hold the action button for 6 seconds, until the light turns orange. If you are having trouble connecting your device to the Wi-Fi unplug the power adapter to reset the device. Plug the power adapter back into the wall and retry setup.

Once you have successfully connected your device to the wireless network, you are ready to use Alexa.

Setting Up Your Echo Show & Echo Spot

Setting up your Echo show or Echo Spot is slightly different when utilizing the screen. After you have unboxed your device and placed it in an area fitting to your needs, plug in the device and let it load. Like with the setup of any Echo device you will need to use your smartphone to navigate to the Alexa Application and log in.

After your device has finished loading, you will see a prompt to complete the Wi-Fi setup on your device's screen. From there you will need to enter in your corresponding network and Amazon Account information. Your device will check for updates upon connecting to the wireless network and begin downloading them automatically.
You will know setup is complete when you see your home screen with the rotating pages.

Setting Up Your Echo Dot (2nd Generation)

Setting up your Echo Dot is extremely like setting up your regular Echo device. Start the process by unboxing and plugging in your Amazon Echo Dot. After successfully opening and logging into the application select "Devices" along the bottom tray of the application. Here you will see already paired devices or groups you have created. To add your new device, you will select the plus sign on the upper right hand corner. When prompted, select "Add Device".

After clicking add device you will need to select your device type and specific device name. After selecting "Echo Dot", you will need to select the generation of your device. If you are unfamiliar with the generation of your device, the varying Dots are pictured on the screen, choose the one which corresponds to the one you have. You will then need to follow the on screen prompts to get your device connected to your wireless network. Your device is ready to connect to the network when your ring light appears orange. Once your device has been connected, it is ready for use.

Setting Up Your Echo Tap

Before beginning setup of your device make sure that you have your charging cable plugged into the charging cradle as well as the wall outlet. Echo Tap is one of Amazon's only portable Alexa devices and it does not directly plug into the wall. Place your device on the charging cradle. You will see the indicators on your Amazon Tap illuminate blue. After roughly a minute, your device will then enter setup mode. You may continue with setup when the front indicators show orange. If you do not see the orange lights you will need to press and hold the Wi-Fi button on the bottom back of the device for 6 seconds.

amazon tap

Front

2.6"

Back

6.2"

| Microphone button | Front light indicators | Power Button | 3.5 mm Audio Input | Micro-USB Power | Bluetooth/ Wi-Fi Button |

You will now need to open your Alexa application and add a new device via the devices tab. You will then be prompted to continue Wi-Fi setup. Once you have completed the guided setup, your device is ready for use.

Unlike the other Echo devices, by default, to give Alexa commands, you will need to press the **Talk** button. When out, to conserve battery, press the power button to enable sleep mode on your device.

You can also opt to set your Tap up for hands free use. This can be done via the Alexa application. From the bottom tray select Devices. Find your device and select it. From there simply press the **Hands-free** option to toggle it on or off.

How to Give Commands to Alexa

Giving Alexa commands is extremely simple and does not require any advanced skills to do. Upon activation of your device she is ready and willing to provide answers to an array of questions which do not require a skill.

To start your interaction, you should tell wake/command word "Alexa". The Echo responds when you begin echo command with 'Alexa'. If you want to stop some operation you should say: "Alexa, stop."

However, to get the information, you need you must remember a few small details when giving commands to Alexa.

1. **Your commands must always start with the wake word.** This allows you device to know when you are speaking to it and expect a response.
2. **Some commands must include the application name.** When your command is specific to a certain skill you must remember to provide the name of the skill to receive relevant information. For example, "Alexa, ask TV Shows what time Family Feud starts."
3. **You must specify which application to play music from otherwise it will play from the default.** If you do not have a

default set it will attempt to play the music from Amazon. "Alexa, play Beyoncé on Apple Music."

4. **Alexa only supports 3 Overall Languages.** Currently Alexa supports 3 languages: German, English and Japanese and provides the ability to support 5 dialects, Australia, Canada, India, UK & the US.

If you are not content using "Alexa" as the wake word for your device. Simply give the command, "Alexa, Change the wake word,". She will then respond with a list of feasible words. You then can respond with the word you have chosen. She will respond confirming the change and you are done.

Changing the word can also be done from within the application through the Settings → Device Settings. You will then need to choose the device which you would like to change the word for and select "wake word".

Getting Acquainted with Alexa Voice Recognition

After you have set up your account you are ready to get acquainted with Alexa. You can do so by setting up a voice profile Creating a voice profile allows you to customize your Alexa experience to fit your needs. Voice profiles are beneficial when using skills like calling and messaging or even shopping. It allows you to play & send messages or even purchase items without an extra authentication step.

To begin this process simply command Alexa by saying, "Alexa, learn my voice". Alexa will then provide a series of commands. It will take anywhere between 15 to 20 minutes for Alexa to learn your voice. If you already have a voice profile setup your device will simply say, "(Name), I already know your voice".

Another way to begin voice recognition is from the Alexa application. From the navigation menu, locate your settings. Within the setting menu there will be an option which reads

"Your Voice". Select this option to begin setting Alexa up to recognize your voice.

Once you click begin, you will be asked to choose the device which you are working to personalize. From there you will be shown 10 different phrases that you must speak back to your device. Wait 15-20 minutes for the recognition to take effect and you are done.

Alexa should now be smart enough to not only know your voice but she will also offer personalized results based on who is speaking. For example, even commands like "Alexa, play music" will output music based on your previous preferences. Voice profiles can be setup for the multiple users on the Echo device.

Setting Up Multiple Echo Users

Setting up your device for your personal use is a breeze however what do you do if you need your device setup for your family? Amazon of course has the answer. Household gives other users the ability to talk to your Alexa device however, they can now use their own Amazon accounts. It also allows you to share select content and access customized information. With your household profile, you can add 1 other adult account to your device.

Before you can begin using this feature you must first set up an Amazon Household, this can be done online or within the

Alexa application. The individual you are attempting to add to your household must also be present to log into their current Amazon account.

1. Open the Alexa application and navigate to the settings area using the menu icon on the top left.
2. Select "Alexa Account" and then select "Amazon Household".

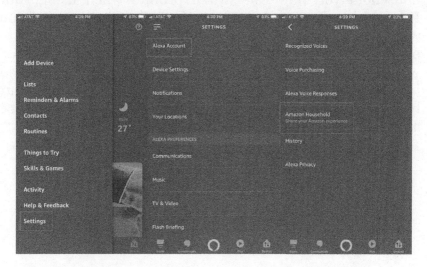

3. The intended user will then need to log into their Amazon account when prompted.

4. After you have verified the user's account they will need to select "Join Household" to agree to Amazon's Terms & Conditions.
5. The new user will now be shown a welcome screen. Continue to follow the on-screen prompts to ensure that the accounts have been set up correctly.

After you have successfully added the new user to your household you now can switch profiles when using your Echo device. By simply saying "Alexa, Switch Accounts" you will be able to use the second adult profile. If you are unsure of which account is in use simply say the command, "Alexa, which account is this?" for her to provide the needed information. Note that when adding a new account to your household if that account is removed neither account will be able to be added to a new household for 180 days.

Chapter 2: How to Setup Echo's Calling & Messaging

To properly set up your device for communication you must have three things. That includes an Amazon account, the Alexa application and a mobile phone number. Although you must have a mobile phone number, all calling is done through your wireless network.

To begin configuring your device open the Alexa application. From within the Alexa application choose "Communicate" from the bottom tray. You will then need to follow the prompts to verify your mobile number. Once your phone number has been verified there are several options available to you.

There are a variety of call types offered through your Alexa device. These types include:

Calling a mobile or landline number: With your Alexa device, you can call not just most mobile or landline numbers in the U.S but in Canada and Mexico as well. This can be handle via the Alexa application or through voice commands to your Echo device. You also have the option to speak the phone number or call a previously added contact.

Device to Device Calling: This type of calling allows people with companionable devices to make and receive calls. For your call to work the other user must have

Communication enabled on their device. This can be done at the device level or via the Alexa application.

After enabling your device for communication, calling is a breeze. To initiate a call via voice simply give Alexa the following command, "Alexa, make a call." She will respond with, "Which number or device would you like to call?"

You will then need to provide the contact name or number which you are attempting to call. If you have multiple numbers for the specified individual, Alexa will ask for clarification on who to call. If you have successfully set up your voice profile the receiving user will see your phone number on their "caller ID". The contacts from your phone will also appear in your Amazon contacts list. You even have the option of importing contacts from other sources.

Amazon also boasts several accessories which can be used to make and receive calls. This includes items like the Echo Connect, which allows you to connect your house phone to your Alexa enabled device to create a speakerphone affect. It would use your current phone service provider to make calls.

It's important to remember that your Echo Device cannot call all numbers. The list below includes numbers which cannot be called by your Echo devices:

- Emergency Numbers or N-1-1 Numbers: This includes 911, 411, 311 or 211
- Numbers which include letters: (1-800-EDISON-1)
- Numbers outside of Canada, US & Mexico
- Toll free numbers or numbers beginning with 1-900

Calling another Alexa device is very like calling a mobile or landline number. To start a call via the Alexa Application, choose a contact from your contacts list. Although confusing, choose the telephone icon to begin a call. This will start a call with the user's Alexa device not the mobile phone if it is connected.

Aside from making phone calls you can also use your Echo device to send SMS messages to mobile numbers or to another Alexa device, however the functionality to have your Echo device read your received SMS messages is still not available.

Sending a message via two Alexa devices is as simple as sending a text message. When using your voice simply command by saying "Alexa, send a message to Billy". She will respond by asking for the contents of the message. Once you are done, Alexa will send your message.

Another avenue for messaging Alexa users is through the Alexa application itself. Simply open your Alexa app, select the communication icon and select the contact you wish to send a message to. The interface within app is like that of a regular text thread.

Once you receive a response to your message, the Echo device will blink yellow until the message is checked as well as receiving a notification on your mobile device. For Alexa to play your message, simply say the command, "Alexa, read my messages.".

Using Drop In

Drop In is a feature that you can use to communicate in and around your household. It can be used as an intercom system for checking in on various rooms rather than calling a specific person. You also have the option to do drop in video on devices which feature a screen, this include the Eco Show or the Echo spot.

To use the Drop-in feature, you must have communication enabled and set up on your device. When attempting a drop in, command Alexa by saying "Alexa, drop in on (speaker name)". This can only be done with any of the devices within your household.

Drop in can also be initiated from your Alexa app like many of Alexa's features. Simply select the "Communicate" option from within the application and tap the Drop-in Icon. You will need to specify which device you would like to drop in on, if you only have one device it will begin the drop-in session.

Amazon has also expanded the ability to use drop in with outside members of your home. In your Messaging and Calling profile there is a setting which manages drop ins. This is used to determine if you can drop in on others and devices within your home. To enable your ability to perform drop ins, follow the steps listed below:

1. Navigate to the Conversation area of the Amazon Alexa application by selecting the communication icon from the bottom tray. Select the contact icon in the top right hand corner of the screen. This is the person icon.
2. Navigate to the contact which you would like to alter and select their name.
3. Toggle the button on the user's contact record for Drop In. This will allow or block permissions on the contact.
4. Drop Ins can also be done on your own devices; however, they must first be enabled on your profile. Click your name at the top of your contacts list. It should read "My Profile & Settings".

Toggle the "Allow Drop In" button to perform drop ins on your own devices.

Blocking Calls & Messages from Your Device

The Do Not Disturb feature gives users the ability to temporarily suspend calling and messaging notifications from coming to their device. This will stop all notifications for calls, messages and even Drop In.

On Echo devices which have a screen simply swipe down from the top and you will see a do not disturb icon. For all other devices, these periods of inactivity can be scheduled from within the Alexa application. To do so select "Devices". From there you will need to select the device which you would like to limit. Select "Do Not Disturb. When turned on you also have the option to select scheduled and create a start and end time for your inactivity.

Chapter 3: Different Types of Echo

Amazon's Echo offers a variety of devices to fit the needs of all users. These devices vary in size, price point and even function. The list continues to grow as Amazon releases new and more innovative items.

The Amazon Echo is a wireless speaker that can become your personal assistant. It has a wide range of functionality that will meet your demands and requirements to make your life easier.

The difference of Echo from Siri and Cortana is the ability to recognize and process voice commands through the Alexa OS, as well as outside a smartphone device. Owing to its omnidirectional speakers and microphones you can activate Amazon Echo from anywhere that Alexa can hear you. After making voice recognition training, Alexa can understand individual users even with an uncommon dialect or accent.

The Amazon Echo (generation 2) brought about a stylish upgrade for the device. It loses it volume dial and gets a top like that of the 2nd generation Echo Dot. It also gains a removable fabric exterior that is available in three colors or can be swapped for a different skin. The sound, although still lacking, can easily be combatted by utilizing a Bluetooth speaker or plugging it into an external speaker via the audio jack.

The second generation Echo also comes fully equipped with 7 microphones as well as noise cancelling technology to ensure you are heard no matter what is playing. These microphones aid in directional and accurate voice detection, which are located at the top of the device.

You can give your commands to the Amazon Echo from another room but for better responsiveness it's recommended to place the device in a central location and at least eight inches from any wall.

If you need to adjust the volume you should use the buttons located on top of the Echo. Then the LEDs will provide visual representation of the volume level. The other way to adjust the volume is to tell Alexa to "turn volume up" or "turn volume down". Or you can adjust more precisely by using a 1 - 10 scale: 1 being very quiet, 10 being very loud. Simply say: "Alexa, volume #" and Alexa will adjust the volume you need. You can also adjust the volume manually. If the Volume is at the highest level, Alexa will try to understand your commands.

The Amazon Echo is always on and listening. In case if you want to prevent the Echo from responding to words not intended as commands, you should simply press the mute microphone button at the top of the device.

There are several devices offered by Amazon outside of the Echo. This list contains the Echo devices currently offered by Amazon.

- Amazon Echo
- Echo Dot
- Echo Show
- Echo Plus
- Echo Dot Kids Edition
- Echo Look
- Echo Spot
- Echo Tap

Aside from the traditional devices, Amazon offers a variety of specialty devices for specific purposes or which include simply includes screens and cameras. These include the Echo Plus, Echo Spot and even the Echo Look.

Echo Plus

The Echo Plus (2nd Generation) is Amazon's advanced edition of the traditional Echo speaker. Although boasting a slightly higher price of $149.99 in comparison to the original Echo at $89.99 the new Echo Plus is a great upgrade. The Echo Plus incorporates room filling sound utilizing its 3" neodymium woofer and 0.8" tweeter as well as a Zigbee hub

Technical details

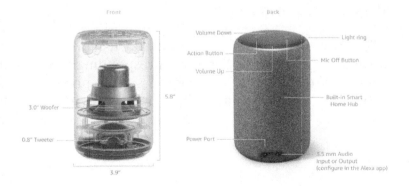

to control smart home devices. It also gives users the ability for line in or out connections as well as Bluetooth.

The new Echo Plus also offers an upgraded design which allows you to choose your color as it is wrapped in fabric much like the Google Home. Options include Charcoal, Heather Grey and Sandstone. It is also shorter and lighter in weight than the original Echo. Amazon has also added a built-in temperature sensor to the new device. This feature allows you to create routines or give Smart Thermostat commands based on the temperature in the home.

Switching things up from the first generation of the Echo, the volume ring is no longer a part of its design.

Echo Show

The 2nd generation of the Echo Show is a voice activated smart assistant which now comes equipped with a 10.1" touchscreen 720 P HD display. It does not follow the traditional cylindrical or puck like design of prior Echo devices. Instead, it is rectangular in the front with a rounded, fabric covered back. The 2nd generation of the Echo Show still comes equipped with a 5 MP camera and 8 microphones which have been dispersed around the device. The speakers have now been moved to the back of the device rather than the front.

Being that this is one of the 2 Amazon devices that is offered with a screen navigation can now be done in three ways; via the touchscreen, the Alexa application and via voice. For example, simple commands like "Alexa, go home" can be vocalized or the user may simply swipe down on the screen and select the home button. Even tasks like scrolling up and down on your screen can be vocalized although swiping the screen may be easier.

Amazon has also added Smart Home control directly to the main drop down of the device allowing users easy access to connected devices. Generation 2 also comes with better sound quality with upgraded 2 inch speakers and a bass radiator. Although the speaker has been upgraded, YouTube is still nowhere to be found.

Echo Look

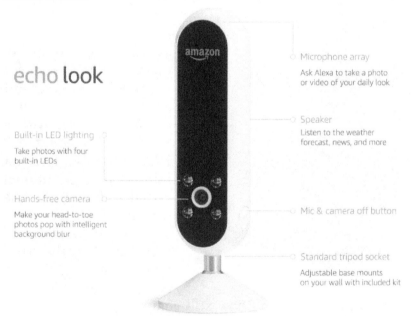

The Echo Look is Amazon's attempt at creating a personal stylish that is available whenever you need it. This device although equipped with Alexa is meant to be used in your bedroom or closet.

The most prominent feature of this device is the hands-free camera which allows you to take full length pictures of your outfit using only your voice. The camera also automatically blurs your background to ensure that your outfit is the highlight of the photo. Simply say, "Alexa, take my picture." And your work is complete.

The Echo look even allows you to create videos of your outfit which are sent directly to your smartphone. In the associated mobile application. This is the perfect tool for influencers or style enthusiasts.
Although the Echo Look is not your typical Echo device and comes equipped with its own person skill, Style Check, it can be directly compared to the Amazon Echo. It boasts no shortage of functions.

Echo Dot (3rd Generation)

The Echo Dot has always been framed as the Echo's little sister. It could perform all the tasks and has all the same features that the Echo has but in a smaller package with lesser sound quality. However, the 3rd generation of the Echo Dot has given the device the boost it needed.

Physically the Echo Dot retains its puck like shape but is slightly larger than the original design. The new Dot received a wider base and an overall heavier design. It also comes equipped with four pin hole microphones compared to the one pin hole mic offered in the previous generations.

Amazon also has wrapped the Echo Dot in a fabric covering which is now offered in 3 different colors (Heather grey, Charcoal & Sandstone). This is an upgrade from the plain shiny black exterior in prior generations.

The speaker also received an upgrade, now harboring a complete 360 degree 1.6-inch speaker.

Under the hood, Alexa is still at its core.

Aside from the release of the 3rd generation Echo Dot, Amazon also rolled out the Echo Dot, Kids Edition. This Echo Dot looks identical to the earlier generations of the Amazon Echo however it has been encased in a hard plastic for durability. This plastic comes in red, green or blue.

This device is a great way to introduce your tech savvy kid to smart assistants. When unboxing, this version of the Echo Dot comes equipped with a comic book style user manual to make it appeal to younger users. Aside from the aesthetics you may be asking yourself what makes this item kid friendly.

One major difference in this version of the Echo Dot is that it filters out explicit music played through Amazon Music, it disables purchasing via voice, provides positive reinforcement to little users and even comes fully equipped with kid friendly knock-knock jokes and alarms. Another major feature of this device is that you, the parent, can utilize parental controls to limit the amount of time kids can use the device as well as the hours which the device can respond.

The Echo Dot Kids comes in at $80 which is $30 more than the standard Echo Dot. The increased pricing is due to the addition of 1 year of FreeTime Unlimited. This gives your child access to educational materials, music and a variety of other media options. It also comes with a 2-year warranty rather than the standard one year warranty with other Eco devices.

Chapter 4: Advanced Functions and Settings of the Amazon Echo

Functions, Fun, and Advanced Settings on Your Echo Dot

This chapter contains all necessary information you need to know about the functions that your Amazon Echo can perform. Here you will also read about advanced settings that this device has.

Music and Media with Your Amazon Echo

The Amazon Echo is famous for its option of listening to music and books. It makes appealing for a great number of users as the Echo has connection with third-party applications and subscription services.

Even you do not have a music subscription you are able to connect the Echo to their library using Alexa.

Listening to Music on Your Alexa Device

The Amazon Echo offers such a great variety of options: listening to podcasts, stream music, audiobooks and adding your music library on Amazon from iTunes, Google Play, and many others.

You can also ask Alexa to stream music from different subscription services. The services may have free and paid music subscriptions.

Here are the following subscription services:
- Amazon Music
- Audible
- iHeartRadio
- Prime Music
- Amazon Music Unlimited
- Spotify Premium
- TuneIn

Upload Music to Your Library

If you want to play your personal music library you should use Amazon Music for PC or Mac to be able to upload your songs into "My Music" section on Amazon. You can upload 250 songs for free but if you want to add more song you must have an Amazon Music Subscription.
Note: If you have free account you cannot buy more than 250 songs via the Digital Music Store for free.

Third-Party Music Services

You can get access to third-party music services by linking your music service account within Alexa. To provide this you should select **Music & Books** from the navigation panel within the app and select the streaming service you want. Once you have selected the desired streaming service you should select **Link Account to Alexa** and sign in with your credentials. Then you will be able to use Alexa with the desired service.

Audible and Kindle Unlimited

It's also possible to use your Echo stream audiobooks and other media. Audible and Kindle can be used with the Amazon Echo. You can read newspaper and magazine audio subscriptions, notes, bookmarks and narration speed controls.
Here are some commands that you can use:
- *"Play [title of work] from Audible."*
- *"Stop reading the book in [60] minutes."*
- *"Play the book, [Huckleberry Finn]."*

LENDING LIBRARY

Alexa can also be helpful for reading items from Amazon Kindle. The books that you have purchased from the Kindle store, the items shared within your Family Library or borrowed from Kindle Unlimited or Kindle Owners' Lending Library are included in eligible books.
For this moment, Alexa is not able to support comics, graphic novels, or narration speed control.
Here are simple commands for Amazon Kindle:
- *"Read my book, [book title]."*
- *"Read my Kindle Book."*

Music Unlimited for Echo Devices

You can listen to a great variety of music on your Echo device if you have the Amazon Music subscription.

You can buy your Amazon Music Unlimited for Echo Subscription with the help of Alexa and your Echo. If you have never had a music subscription, you can get free trial via voice commands.

You should know that the free trial takes $1 for your account and it will be removed within 72 hours.

You should tell "Sign up for Amazon Music Unlimited" to complete the signing up for a music subscription via Alexa. And Alexa will help you with this procedure.

Flash Briefings

You can get updates from popular broadcasters, the latest headlines from the Associated Press and weather information with the help of flash briefing.

But first you must customize your settings within the Alexa app. You can have these things customized: shows, weather updates, headlines. It is also possible to edit the order in which the program plays in your flash briefings.

You can view more flash briefing content if you use the "Get More Flash Briefing Content". You also have such option

when Alexa has read the flash brief you can also read the full stories as the link will appear in your Alexa application.
Here are simple commands for your Flash Briefing:

- *"What's new?"*
- *"What's my flash briefing?"*

Sports Updates

You can get the results of the latest scores and game information for your teams by asking Alexa. But first you should set up them in the Alexa app to enable this feature.

Just select **Settings** > **Sports** and add your sport teams from the Alexa app. Then you should enter the name of your favorite sports team into the search field and you will see the suggestions of the team names.

So, when you want to hear your sports updates, tell Alexa *"Give me my Sports Update"*.

Weather Forecast

If you need to know weather forecast every day, your Echo can help you with it. It can give local weather forecasts as well as the weather in any city of U.S. You should just add your address in the Alexa app to provide more accurate forecast.

You can easily edit the information from the Alexa settings menu and change your location.

Using the Alexa app, you can get a seven-day forecast when you ask Alexa about the weather. Usually Alexa takes the information from AccuWeather to provide the weather forecast.

Here is the list of phrases you can use to know your weather forecast:

- What's the weather today?
- What's the weather for tomorrow?
- What's the weather for this weekend?

Traffic Requests

If you want to set up traffic updates in Alexa, first, you must have a travel route set within the app. Your starting location is usually associated with the address you have entered in your Amazon account.

You can update your traffic conditions according to your desired route and its duration with the help of Alexa. To provide updates just select **Settings** > **Traffic** from your Alexa app and update "from" and "to" address.

Here are the phrases to ask Alexa about traffic updates:

- *"How is traffic?"*
- *"What's my commute?"*

Nearby Locations

If you don't know which restaurant to choose tonight or where to do shopping in your area your Amazon Echo Dot

will find it for you. To provide this Alexa usually uses your device location in combination with Yelp. Alexa is ready to help you with any searches to find exactly what you need. Your Amazon Echo can find top-rated businesses, business hours and phone numbers, different business types and to get the addresses of nearby business.

Movie Showtimes

Alexa is also able to find movies and movie show times as your address is already set up in the Alexa app. You need to use your cell phone, Alexa will do it for you. While searching for specific theatres and movies Alexa uses IMDb.

Using your Echo, you can find out what movies are playing near you, movies playing in other cities as well as specific show times. You can also be more specific with your requests by asking to find specific show times at a specific theater.

Ask Alexa

The Amazon Echo can answer almost all your question concerning world, people, dates, history, geography, trivia and many others. Alexa can even do some simple calculations, spell words or define them.

Here are useful phrases:

- *"Who is [person name]?"*
- *"Who starred in the TV Show [title]?"*
- *"When is [holiday]?"*
- *"Who starred in the Movie [title]?"*

Productivity

This amazing device can become a great assistant for a person who needs planning, making to-do lists, updating his calendars. Amazon Echo is a little organizer which can wake you up, to give updates on the nearest events and necessary tasks, and many other options.

Timers and Alarms

Alexa can also help with setting multiple timers or alarms. You can set up timers and alarms to 24 hours ahead of time.

If you have already set up alarm with your voice you can edit it inside the Alexa app. Besides, you can make new alarms, turn them on or off, using the Alexa app.

The Alexa app can perform three functionalities. You can change your alarm volume, alarm sound or delete an alarm

Here are the voice commands for alarms:
- *"Set a repeating alarm for [day of week] at [time]."*
- *"Wake me up at [time]."*
- *"What alarms do I have?"*

You can get a great variety of functionality with timers. But you can pause, resume your timer or change your timer volume only by using the Alexa app.

You should remember that you cannot change timer's volume using the device volume as they work independently.

Here is the list of voice commands that you can use with timers:
- *"Set the timer for [time]."*
- *"Set a timer for [x amount of time]."*

Manage Lists

If you have a great list of important tasks every day then Amazon Echo is ready to help you with it. You should know that each list must not exceed 100 items and each item must not contain more than 256 characters.

You can open your shopping and to-do lists through the Alexa app, the Amazon app and the Alexa Shopping list. Alexa is also able to add some item to your shopping or to-do list and review it when you use your Echo.

Besides, Alexa can link the third-party list services. Let's see this option in details.

Linking Third-Party List Services to Your Echo

This option is useful as it helps to manage tasks and things that you need to remember. Your Echo should be used with third-party list services to provide this option.

If you want to activate this option you should link the service in the Alexa app. So, go to the **Settings** > **Lists** to see the desired list service. Then you should enter your login or create a new account. You can use the screen prompts to complete your setup.

Adding or Reviewing Calendar Events

Your Echo can also help you if you want to add or review events in your Google Calendar. But, first, you must link your Google Calendar within the Alexa app to start using the calendar features.

To activate this option, go to **Settings** > **Email & Calendar** >**Add Account** and select **Google**. Then select the desired toggle for email or calendar, by default both are chosen. Select **Connect Account** and you will be prompted to log into your desired Google account.

Here are the phrases for managing your calendar:

- *"What's on my calendar on [day]?"*

- *"When is my next event?"*
- *"Add [event] to my calendar for [day] at [time]."*

Using Voicecast to Send Content

You can also use your Echo to send details about news, weather and other things to your Fire tablet. You just need to turn on Automatic Voicecast and you will be able to send the content to your Fire tablet automatically.

You will see the notification on the lock screen of the tablet that the content has been sent to your Fire tablet. When you unlock the device, you will see the notification in the Quick Settings menu of your Fire tablet.

Voicecast also include a lot of Alexa features such as:

- Music
- Questions and answers
- Flash Briefing
- Lists
- Weather
- Timer and alarms
- Wikipedia
- Help

If you want to ask Alexa about something, simply say *"Send that to [device name]"* or *"Show this on my Fire tablet"*.

Shopping and Placing Orders with Alexa

You can also do shopping using your Echo. You can buy music, order an Alexa device, or place orders using Alexa.
When you need to make a purchase, Alexa can search through various purchase options which include:

- Your order history: You can order only Prime-eligible items using Alexa.
- Prime-eligible items: They include items which are eligible for delivery by Prime now.
- Amazon's Choice: You can choose some items which has high rating and good price with Prime shipping.

Purchasing with Alexa is easy as she usually tells the item name and price before purchasing. She can also provide additional shipping information in case the purchase will not be delivered through Amazon Prime. Then Alexa will ask you either to confirm or cancel the order.

Alexa also have additional options which make shopping on Amazon more convenient. She can add items to your cart, add items to an Alexa Shopping list or you can ask for more information if the item cannot be found or you cannot complete the purchase.

You should also set up some requirements on your Amazon account to be able to place an order using your Alexa device.

If you want to make an order from the Digital Music Store you should have annual Prime Membership. You must have Amazon account and a payment method must be set up in 1-click settings. The same requirements are for purchasing physical products.

You can navigate your shopping setting through the Alexa app. You can turn off voice purchasing or require a confirmation code before every order.

Here are the commands for purchasing Prime-eligible items:

- *"Order an [item name]."* If Alexa has found the product you should say yes/no to confirm.
- *"Reorder [item name]."* If Alexa has found the product you should say yes/no to confirm.
- *"Add [item name] to my cart."* Alexa will add an item to your cart on Amazon.
- *"Cancel my order."* Alexa will cancel an order immediately.

If you purchase some music maybe you will need a confirmation code before initiating a purchase. This will prevent from purchasing music on your account by someone else.

You should use the following commands to buy music:

- *"Shop for the song [song name]."*
- *"Shop for the album [album name]."*
- *"Buy this [song]." You can use* this command if some song is playing on an Amazon-supported station.

Tracking Orders with Your Echo

Using your Echo, you can also track your orders via Alexa. If you have more than one active order, Alexa will give you information about the order with a delivery date that is closest to the current date
Here are the phrases to track your orders:
- *"Where is my stuff?"* or *"Track my order"*

After these phrases, Alexa will give you information about your orders.

Amazon Echo also can serve as a hub for your home control. It is able to control your lights, different switches around your home, your thermostat, such items like Phillips, Hive, or Hue devices. You will get to know how to control your smart home in the following chapters.

Fun Phrases to Try Out with Alexa

Here is the list of funny phrases you can try for your Echo or any device with Alexa. There are even more phrases that Amazon Alexa development team has put into Alexa. Check them out:
Alexa, who's your daddy?

Alexa, I am your father.
Alexa, all your bases belong to us.
Alexa, Romeo, Romeo wherefore art thou Romeo?
Alexa, beam me up.
Alexa, how many roads must a man walk down?
Alexa, who lives in a pineapple under the sea?
Alexa, what is the meaning of life?
Alexa, what is the loneliest number?
Alexa, how much is that doggie in the window?
Alexa, define rock, paper, scissors, lizard, Spock.
Alexa, how much wood can a woodchuck chuck if a woodchuck could chuck wood?
Alexa, Earl Grey. Hot. (or Alexa, tea. Earl Grey. Hot.)
Alexa, what does the Earth weigh?
Alexa, when is the end of the world?
Alexa, make me a sandwich.
Alexa, do you have a boyfriend?
Alexa, do you want to build a snowman?
Alexa, do you really want to hurt me?
Alexa, what is the best tablet?
Alexa, which comes first: the chicken or the egg?
Alexa, may the force be with you.
Alexa, what is your favorite color?
Alexa, who won best actor Oscar in 1973?
Alexa, what is your quest?
Alexa, do aliens exist?

Alexa, how many licks does it take to get to the center of a Tootsie pop?
Alexa, what are you going to do today?
Alexa, where do you live?
Alexa, what is the airspeed velocity of an unladen swallow?
Alexa, where do babies come from?
Alexa, what is love?
Alexa, who is the real Slim Shady?
Alexa, who let the dogs out?
Alexa, open the pod bay doors.

What's New for Alexa & the Echo Family

One of Alexa's biggest attractions is that it will get better with time, no matter what version of the physical Echo you have. It is continuously updated and your device continues to get smarter. There are several upgrades which have been rolled out to not just the Echo products but the Alexa App as well. The list below contains new and interesting updates made by Amazon.

If you have been an Alexa user for a bit of time now you would have noticed that the mobile application has transformed into something easier to use and overall more aesthetically pleasing. It makes adding device, changing settings and even communicating with your Echo device much easier.

Amazon also upgraded the way you connect devices to your WI-FI network with an option they are calling Wi-Fi Simple Setup. This allows you to simple command Alexa to discover your devices. It will then use the information that it already knows to add the new device.

Brief Mode & Follow Up Mode

Brief mode allows users to hear less of Alexa voice and provides instead beeps for confirmations. Brief Mode was introduced to give users a quicker alternative to commands and confirmations. For simple messages, Alexa will chime when this mode is toggled. One additional feature introduced with Brief Mode is Follow Up Mode. Follow Up Mode allows you to talk to Alexa in a more conversational manner without constantly repeating the wake word. This can be helpful when needing to add successive items to a to do list or shopping list.

Apple Music

One major change that Amazon introduced is the integration with Apple music. Previously, users could only use Spotify, Amazon Music, TuneIn or IHeartRadio as their default music services however Apple Music has been added to this list. To begin using Apple Music you will need to enable the skill and log into your Apple account from within the Alexa application. If for some reason your Apple Music skill is not working try enabling the app again and making sure you have chosen "Allow" on the Apple authentication page as well as that you have enabled the skill.

Once this is completed you can then ask Alexa to play specific music and even playlists. However, Apple isn't the only music streaming app which will allow this feature. Command Alexa by saying, "Alexa, play [Top Hits] playlist from [Spotify]," to play a specific playlist.

Location Based Routines

Aside from the more obvious changes to your Echo device, Amazon has also introduced a series of location based routines which can activate whenever your reach a certain location or destination. The location readings are taken from your smartphone and allow you to do things like turn off all the lights when you leave home or lock the doors automatically. Reminders can also be handled in the same manner. Alexa also introduced a feature which provides the ability to check your email and provide a summary of all new messages.

Alexa Guard is a new feature that can be used whenever you leave our home. To activate this feature, you need to say "Alexa, I'm leaving". When this skill is active you will get alerts if Alexa hears suspicious noises which include breaking glass, smoke detectors or carbon monoxide alarms from within your home. If connected to smart devices she can also flicker lights and activate alarm systems, with the necessary integrations.

Local Control is another new feature which allows users to have control over smart home devices like lights, plugs and switches if you have an unreliable internet connection or temporary outage.

Whisper Mode allows users to whisper to Alexa and have her respond back in a whisper voice to be sure not to wake sleeping family members.

Chapter 5: The Echo/Echo Dot Voice Remote

The official remote is necessary for the Echo and Echo Dot to connect the devices via Bluetooth. The remote is 5.5 inches long and 1.5 inches wide. When you are far away from Alexa or the room is too noisy you can use the integrated microphone in the remote. The remote can be used from any room in your house and on the distance up to 100+ feet away. The buttons of remote can move to the next or previous track, play or pause, and control the volume of the device(s). The remote can work with only one Echo device at a time and it is not compatible with the Amazon Tap or the Fire TV.

The remote uses 2 AAA which are available with the setup right out of the box. Later you will need to change them but it may be a little difficult for you to remove the battery cover to replace the batteries. You should follow these steps to remove the battery cover easily: hold the remote face down in the palm of your hand with the top pointed away from you. Then you should find the battery cover tab, indicated by that is the inside of an equal sign, and using something hard, but not sharp, press down on the tab while also pulling the bottom of the cover up. It is not so difficult as it seems for the first time.

You can get the instructions from the Alexa app in the *Device Settings* menu option if they are not included with the remote. You should select the device that you want to pair it with and then select Echo Remote under the **Connected Device** heading. Then it will ask you to press and hold the play button on the remote for a few seconds until it's been detected. Once it's detected you can use it.

If you need to activate the voice control you should press and hold the mic button while you speak. In this case means you don't need to use your chosen wake word (Alexa, Amazon, or Echo) with the remote. While holding the mic button, just say your command *"Turn on kitchen"* and depending on the skill you've setup, the kitchen lights will be turned on. You should know that you will need to hold the mic button for the whole command to be heard and understood. If you just press and release while speaking you will not manage to activate the voice control.

As you know, you can enable the remote only for one device at a time. But if you would like to pair a second remote to be able to have one in different parts of the house, you should go to the Alexa app and choose **Settings** > **Device Settings** > **Designated Device** > **Bluetooth Devices> Pair a new device.**

When the pair process gets started, you should press the play button on the second remote for about 5 seconds until you see it as an *Unknown Device* in the device list. When you connect the Echo to it, it seems like pairing another Bluetooth speaker, but this is the second remote. You will not see the second remote anywhere in the Bluetooth device list but both remotes will then work with that Echo device. That means you can use remotes with one Echo device or pair each remote with its own Echo device.

When you are in a noisy room or the volume is, loud Alexa may not be able to hear, and understand what you say. You can use the remote to pause or stop the music or loud volume. When it is quiet enough you can control the device by speaking to it.

Chapter 6: Alexa Skills & IFTTT

To give your Echo device added functionality and include features which may not be available on your device yet use IFTTT aka If This Then That. This allows you to connect a variety of applications, websites and third party platforms using your Echo device. It's an automation service that enables to connect many your things through the Internet. You can configure the settings using your mobile device or using IFTTT website.

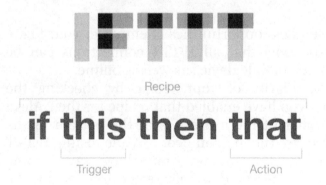

IFTT is a mobile application and a website that works with Phillips Hue systems, Alexa, and many other applications. If you have Smart Home items IFTTT can automate everything from it to simple notifications on your phone.

You should use IFTTT application with Alexa to setup recipes that you can use with the following applications:

- Phillips Hue
- Google Drive
- Todoist
- Gmail
- Evernote
- Google Calendar
- Nest
- Harmony

IFTTT can give endless opportunities to empower your Echo. You should also know that all IFTTT connections can be uploaded through a mobile device as well as online.

You can the popularity of your recipe by checking the number of users who have enabled that recipe for their Alexa device. The number of these users is at the bottom of the recipe card next to the person icon. While using IFTTT online you can see how many people have saved some recipes. You can understand if this recipe is good by the number of people who have saved it.

There is an 'Activity Log' under the notifications selection button that shows when the recipe was run. So, you can receive alerts when the recipe is run.

Using the "My Applets" screen you can monitor your applets or actions activity. If you select 'All' or 'Activity' you will see all the applets or actions that you have turned configured in the past. It will also show you when each of your applets was created and when, if any, were turned off. You can also see when any services were connected to your account.

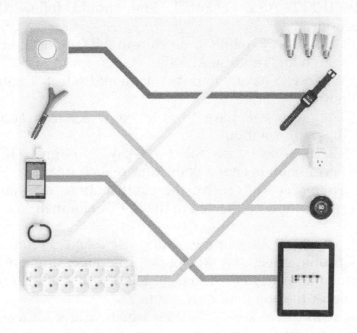

Connecting to the Alexa channel in IFTTT

With IFTTT, users can create recipes, formulas for use, which link to numerous services or other devices, channels, to enhance basic skills. Recipes are made up of triggers and actions. These actions can range from turning on a light to adjusting the temperature in your home. The trigger will generally take place on a platform separate from that of the action. For example, you could create a recipe that states when my alarm goes off, turn on my coffee maker. IFTTT also allows users to create recipes which are triggered by voice commands.

To get started using your Alexa device with IFTTT you must first create an account. Once your account

has been successfully set up you are ready to begin creating personalized recipes.

To be able to stay current with all the preset options for the Alexa and connect to the options available to you connect to the IFTTT Alexa channel. You should follow these instructions:

1. Go to IFTTT online or on your mobile application and search for "Amazon Alexa"
2. When you have found it, you should select "Connect" button.
3. Then you will have to enter your Amazon account login information.
4. Then you must select "Okay" to give IFTTT Permission to access your Amazon account.
5. Then you will receive the confirmation that you are successfully connected to the IFTTT channel.

You can now you can create and use recipes. From your IFTTT profile select "My Recipes". To create a new recipe, select the plus sign in the top right hand corner of the screen and wait for the app options to load.

You will then see a button which reads, "Create A Recipe". Select this button to continue with recipe creation and hooking up the Alexa App with IFTTT. Follow the on-screen tutorial to create integrate the Alexa service.

Once you have selected Alexa as your starting service, you will be able to choose from a list of voice command triggers. Your voice command will depend solely on the task which you would like to create. If none of these options fit your needs, you also have the option to "Say a Specific Phrase" to fit your trigger. This serves as the "If this..." portion of your recipe.

Once you select "done" you will be prompted for the "then that..." portion. Click the plus option to be given a list of available services which your trigger can be connected to.

IFTTT play the role of a central hub which helps to create and to use recipes to run your smart home with. The web-based service IFTTT and Alexa can work with such applications like SmartThings, Phillips Hue, and Harmony. This service allows Alexa to perform the following actions: changing the light color, toggling device power, turning lights on and locking doors. Use the following samples to get acquainted with IFTTT.

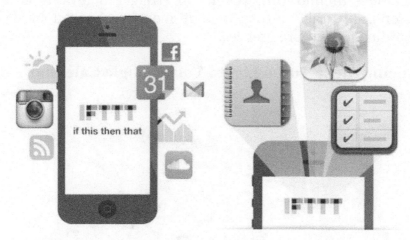

The following instructions concern how to configure Alexa to find your phone:

- You should search 'Amazon Alexa' within the IFTTT application and then you will be shown a list of the already preset Alexa functions.
- Then you should select "Tell Alexa to find my phone" from the list of pre-set recipes.
- Then tap the "Turn On" button to get started with setup.
- You will also be prompted to accept the permissions needed for the trigger to function correctly.
- After you have accepted the permissions you should enter a phone number. When the "Send Pin" button is selected this number will be called. This pin will also be used to verify the call information that will be used when Alexa gets instructions to find the device.

- When you have entered your call information you will receive a confirmation that the phone call has been selected.

After configuration, trigger this recipe when you need to find your phone. Simply tell Alexa to find your phone. And then you will receive a call with a default message of, "Alexa attempted to find your phone on [trigger date]". It is a customizable call message and it may be changed based according to your preferences.

Syncing Alexa To Do List to Your Google Calendar

You can connect a lot of devices with your Echo using IFTTT. The other function for IFTTT and Alexa is syncing your Alexa To Do list with your Google Calendar.

1. You should search 'Amazon Alexa' within the IFTTT application and then you will be shown a list of the already preset Alexa functions.
2. You should select "Automatically sync Alexa to-dos to your Google calendar" from the list of pre-set recipes.
3. Then you should select 'OK' to give IFTTT the needed permissions to access to Google Calendar.
4. To connect your Google Account with IFTTT you should select the Google Account you would like to use with your Alexa to do list and select 'Allow'.

5. Now Alexa is connected to your Google account through IFTTT and it will automatically sync your to-do list items with the calendar.

Alexa & Phillips Hue Lighting

Alexa is able to work with many smart home devices. And one of these devices is Phillips Hue Lighting. You can also add voice commands to your lighting system using Alexa and IFTTT.

The following instructions should help you not only setting up IFTTT, Alexa and Hue lighting, but they will teach you how to successfully connect your hue with trigger commands. Follow these steps:

1. You should search 'Amazon Alexa' within the IFTTT application. Then you will be shown a list of the already preset Alexa functions.
2. Then you should select "Tell Alexa to start the party and put your Hue lights on a color loop" from the list of pre-set recipes.
3. Then select 'OK' to give IFTTT the needed permissions to access to Phillips Hue.
4. Then you will be prompted to log into your Hue Account or to create a new one.

5. You will also receive a notification that your mobile device may now be used to control you Hue lighting.
6. Then you will be sent back to the IFTTT application to configure the settings for your command.
7. You are also able to change the trigger phrase for the recipe within the configurations and select which lights will function on command.
8. When you have completed your desired configurations, you should select the check mark.

You cannot imagine how many activities Alexa is able to perform with Hue Lights. It is able to change the lighting based on song. Alexa can also change the lights when items are added to the to-do list and even make your lights blink when your timer hits zero.

Custom IFTTT Recipes

Except using the preset recipes as listed above you are also able to create recipes from scratch. You should select "Applet Maker" from within the Amazon Alexa channel and you can start creating your own recipes. You can see the button listed under "Try making your own Applet from scratch".

1. When the next screen loads, you should select the '+' sign next to the word "this".
2. Then choose Amazon Alexa as your trigger service.

3. There is a list of triggers that you may use based on the functions of Alexa which is on the next page.

4. When you have chosen your trigger then you will be brought back the previous "If this then that" screen or asked to configure the specific item selected.

5. Now you should see the icon for your If function on the applet maker screen. If it is not there, you should repeat steps 1-4.

6. Then select the '+' sign next to the word 'that' to create the action for your recipe.

7. You will see the list of services offered through the IFTTT app once again. You should select the service for your desired action.

8. Then you should complete the configuration of the action, based on the chosen service. When the action is complete, you should finish your action by selecting the check mark, in the top right hand corner of the screen.

9. When your recipe is complete you will see a summary of your new action. Then select 'Finish' if you are satisfied with the result.

10. Then you will receive a notification message that your new action will be set to 'On'.

In case you have forgotten about recipe you can just select "Check Now" to make sure it is set up correctly.

One of the main functions of IFTTT is its ability to chain multiple recipes together in one bundle. It enables you to give Alexa a command and trigger multiple actions.

IFTT is a necessary tool for your Amazon Echo to automate and control your everyday tasks. If it seems hard to configure your recipes for the first time, soon you will get used to customizing your own recipes and instructions.

Alexa Skills

Alexa skills are a large part of what makes the Amazon Echo function in its intended manor. They give the user functionality that you normally would not expect from a "blue tooth speaker". There are a variety of categories that the Alexa skills fall under. These include games, music & audio, news, kids, Food & drink, productivity and health & fitness.

The skills give you the ability to do things like check your credit card balances using the Capital One application, order food via Pizza Hut and Wing Stop skills and even order an Uber via your Amazon device.

There are thousands of Alexa skills with new skills being added to Alexa's arsenal every day. Using Alexa skills are easy and they can be enabled via your device or via the Alexa Application. Although most skills can be set up using only your voice that is not the case for all skills.

When using the Alexa application, select the menu navigation from the top left and choose "Skills & Games". This will take you to the main interface for Alexa skills. Here you can select the magnifying glass to search for your desired skill or search through the categories offered.

Skills may also be added via the Amazon website. If you see a skill which draws your attention while browsing via the web, simply log into the account which is associated with your Alexa device and enable the skill. It should then be ready for use on your Amazon device.

It's important to remember that many skills from third-party sites like Pandora, Capital One, Spotify, Uber etc. require that you log into your account before the skills will work properly.

Alexa & the Home
Smart Locks & Alexa

The largest draw of the Echo smart assistant devices is the ability to control your home and appliances. The Alexa skills aid in the automation of a multitude of manual everyday functions. These include things like locking and unlocking doors, starting your coffee maker and even recording video for your home.

Alexa even works with a series of deadbolts and locks which can be used for locking and unlocking doors around your home. An array of smart locks is currently sold which work with your Amazon Echo device. Some of these brands include

- Kwikset
- Yale
- Schlage
- SmartThings

To get started with using your Smart home lock you will need three things, we will be using the SmartThings lock as a sample. The needed items include your echo device, the smart lock and the SmartThings Hub/app.

Before beginning to set up your lock via the Alexa companion app you must first connect your lock to the SmartThings Hub. After you have added your device to the SmartThings hub you are ready to install it on your desired door.

After your lock has been setup with SmartThings and installed open your Alexa app and select Devices from the bottom tray. Choose the plus sign located in the upper right hand corner and select Lock from the list. You will then need to choose the specific lock which belongs to you.
You will be prompted to enable to the Skill corresponding to your device and follow the on-screen prompts. After your lock has been successfully installed and found via your device you can now utilize the lock commands for your device.

Door locking commands include:

"Alexa, lock the back door."
"Alexa, is the front door locked."
"Alexa, unlock the side door."

When attempting to lock, unlock or even check the status of a door you must specify the name of the door as you have titled it within the SmartThings application.

Smart Thermostats & Alexa

Aside from using Alexa to lock and unlock your doors, she can also be used to control your thermostat. After connecting your thermostat in a similar manner to the lock mentioned above you are ready to start sending commands to your Alexa device. The list below shows the most commonly used commands when interacting with your Alexa device.

Setting your Nest Temperature
- "Alexa, set the [living room] temperature to [80] degrees.
- "Alexa, turn my [bedroom] temperature to [65] degrees.

Increasing or decreasing Room Temperatures
- "Alexa, make the [living room] warmer by 20 degrees."
- "Alexa, increase the [bedroom] temperature."

There are also a variety of 3rd party Alexa skills which give more flexibility to your Nest experience. For example, users may say things like "Alexa, tell the [bedroom] thermostat that I am too cold."

Appliances & Alexa

Did you know Alexa can control your appliances? There are a host of dishwashers, coffee makers and even vacuums which you can use Alexa to command. Robot vacuums are the latest trend and its therefore only right that you your Alexa functions with them.

If you are using a Wi-Fi connected Roomba with your Alexa device there are several commands you can use to get your Roomba cleaning without lifting a finger.

Start/Stop/Resume Cleaning

- *"Alexa, tell Roomba to begin vacuuming"*
- *"Alexa, tell Roomba to stop cleaning"*
- *"Alexa, tell Roomba to pause cleaning"*

If you have multiple Roombas set up you will need to specify using the name of the robot you would like to perform the task.

- *"Alexa, ask Roomba to have [Bedroom Robot] begin cleaning".*

Aside from simply asking your Roomba to start or stop cleaning you can also get a variety of status updates from your device regarding location and even scheduled cleaning sessions.

- *"Alexa, ask Roomba where it is located."*
- *"Alexa, ask Roomba to schedule a cleaning for [Thursday] at [9AM]."*
- *"Alexa, ask Roomba to go home."*

Parental Controls

Amazon FreeTime allows parents to control their child's activity and access on their Alexa enabled device. Once FreeTime has been enabled through the Alexa companion application parents can disable features, place a block on explicit content and set daily time limits for browsing online, watching videos and reading books. Parents also have the ability manually approve Alexa device skills or audio books.

FreeTime although offering a free version also has a paid version which give more access to an abundance of functionality. This is considered FreeTime Unlimited. It comes in at a price of $119 annually or $4.99 - $9.99 depending on the number of children utilizing the services.

Chapter 7: How to Overcome the Disadvantages of the Echo

As you know, every device has its advantages and disadvantages. Here you will find the common issues with the Amazon Echo and how you can fix them.

- Echo Responsiveness
  This complaint concerns the case when you have noticed that your Amazon Echo has got the lack of responsiveness or the proximity to your Echo so it could pick up your voice.

  You can fix this issue if you re-run your voice training. If you haven't done it before then this is the reason why the Echo is not picking up your speech pattern or voice. Following these steps below, you can run your voice training:
  1. Enter the Alexa app from your smart device.
  2. Select **Settings** > **Alexa Account** > **Recognized Voices** in the Alexa app
  3. Select **Learn my voice**
  4. Then select **Next** and you will be prompted to read aloud 25 phrases. While pronouncing these phrases, speak in your normal tone and also stand or sit your typical distance when you use your Echo. If you have made your voice training right it will not awaken when you are across the room.

- Unexpected Device Limitations

You already know that the Alexa app can perform a lot of activities with the Echo Dot device. But to provide its proper work you must download the necessary skills within the Alexa application.

You can find all of the skills and features on the Alexa Help Page on Amazon.com. The functionality of Alexa is continuously growing. The developers are making more apps to function with Alexa every day.

If you need Alexa to perform specific tasks which are necessary for your everyday life you should know if Alexa can perform such tasks. In case if you purchase this device, you could avoid unexpected limitations. You should make sure that Alexa is able to correspond your needs.

The advantage of working with IFTTT enables this device to connect to a variety of applications that Alexa may not be directly compatible with alone.

- Issues with the Alexa App

  The developers of Alexa constantly update the Alexa app to make each of the Alexa devices more responsive and smarter. If you have got a message that says, "The Alexa app is offline," you can fix it with a number of common solutions.

Here they are:

1. **Restarting your device**: When an Alexa error occurs, you should restart your device. You should long press the sleep/wake button from your iPhone until the option appears on your screen to restart. You can do the same from an Android device, you should hold down your power button until the restart option appears on the screen.

2. **Force close the application**: In order to force close an application from your iPhone you should double press your Home button. Then you will see a slider of open applications on your screen. Then you should swipe the Alexa app upward to close it.

   Then navigate to the *Settings* on your device and select *Apps* or *Applications* from your Android device. You should find Alexa in the list of installed applications. You can clear data for your application if it is necessary. Amazon writes it is recommended to clear the data and select *Force Stop*.

3. **Uninstall the Application**: If you want to remove the application from your phone you should go to the Android device settings, select *Manage applications* and find Alexa in the listing of apps on your device. Then select *Uninstall.* You can also uninstall the application by long pressing on the Alexa app from your general applications section. When you have selected the app, you should drag it to the top of the screen which should read *Uninstall* on the top left. Then press long the Alexa application from your iOS device until it begins to shake on your screen. When it starts shaking tap the 'X' on the app.

After the uninstallation of the application you should navigate to your respective app store and re-download the application

- Echo is not responding to the wake word "Alexa."
  If you have completed the voice training but your Echo is not responding when you say "Alexa" you should open the Alexa app and navigate to **Settings** and select **Device Settings> Desired Device> Wake Word.** In this app, you can change the wake word to or from "Alexa".
- Echo cannot find my music or open the correct application.
  When you give some command to Alexa you must be always specific in what you need. Alexa can perform a lot of commands within the moment but if you have not spoken it properly the Echo will not know how to perform your request.

If you have such issues you should go through the Voice Training section which is described in this guide. It should help you to find commands that you did not know how to use. When you need Alexa to play music it requires specific instructions. Here are the examples:

- *"Play Sting on Spotify."* It is necessary to specify the name of application. Otherwise, Alexa may become confused and it will cause the command to fail. This command is able to shuffle music by this artist from Spotify.
- *"Play Spotify."* If Alexa gets this command it simply plays music where you last left off.

If you have purchased some music from the Digital Music Store or you have connected your personal music library you should give simple commands:

- *"Alexa, play Beyoncé."*
- *"Alexa, play the new Shakira song."*
- *"Alexa, shuffle Michael Jackson."*
Here are other commands to control your music:
- *"Repeat this song,"*
- *"Next song"*
- *"Buy this song"*

Chapter 8: Troubleshooting Issues with the Amazon Echo

This chapter will help you to find some quick answers to common issues if you are having some trouble with the Echo. In case if don't know what to do with troubleshooting, make sure you follow the right steps to fix any issues.

Your Amazon Echo Ring

Your Echo Device Doesn't Connect to the Wi-Fi Network

To ensure the right work of your Amazon Echo, check your Wi-Fi network that it meets the standards of dual-band Wi-Fi (2.4 GHz/5 GHz) networks that use the 802.11a/b/g/n.
The current status of your Wi-Fi network is showed by the power LED on your Echo. You can place the power LED near the power adapter port on the device.

Power LED State	Description
Solid white light	Echo device is connected to your Wi-Fi network
Solid orange light	Echo device is not connected to your Wi-Fi network

Blinking orange light	Echo device is connected to your Wi-Fi network, but it can't access the Alexa Voice Service.

The ring of the Amazon Echo is an indicator if something is wrong with the device. It may have six different color depending on the action.

Here is the description of each color:

Solid Blue and Cyan: You can see these colors after the wake word is spoken, during performing of the user's command and during Alexa's response to your command. While the initial boot process of your Echo is going on you can see these colors.

Solid Red: A red light on your Echo will appear if you select the mute button on the top of your Dot. And this light means your Echo is on Mute.

Orange Spinning Clockwise: If you see this color it means that Echo is trying to connect to the wireless network.

White: If you are adjusting the volume on your device this color usually appears.

Wavering Violet: If your Echo's ring has wavering violet color that means some error has happened during the setup of your wireless network.

In case if you have troubles with starting Echo, try to follow actions:
➤ Restart your Wi-Fi network again.
➤ Make sure you enter the right network password (if required). If you see a lock icon, it means that a network password is required. This password is not your Amazon account password.
➤ You should also verify if other devices, such as tablets or mobile phones can connect to your network. If not, the problem may be with your Wi-Fi network. To solve this problem, you should contact your Internet service provider, network administrator, or the person

who set up your network. They should help you with it.

> You should update the firmware for your router or modem hardware.
> In case if you saved your Wi-Fi password to Amazon, but you decided to change it, you need to re-enter your new Wi-Fi password to connect again.
> In some situations, by default, your router may use both WPA+WPA2 for security. You can solve this problem with connection if you switch the router security type to either WPA or WPA2 only. If the router also has an option to set the type of encryption, you should set it only to AES.

Another tip is to reduce Wi-Fi congestion

> You may have inconsistent Wi-Fi performance when you have multiple devices on your Wi-Fi network.
> You should turn off devices that you aren't using to free up bandwidth on your network.

➤ You should move your device closer to your router and modem if it's blocked by an object.

➤ You should make sure that there are no other sources of possible interference, such as microwave ovens or baby monitors.

➤ **Optional:** You can connect to your router's 5 GHz Wi-Fi frequency band (if it's available). Many Wi-Fi devices only connect to the 2.4 GHz band. If you have many devices that use this band on your network, your network speed may be slower. But you can connect to the less congested 5 GHz band to get better range and less interference.

Issues with Sound

If your Echo is having some issues with sound quality then you can try the following things to solve this issue. One of the reasons is may be an accent. Alexa is able to understand and get acclimated to your voice.

If while giving some command to Alexa you see that Alexa is misconstruing your words you should attempt to run the voice training program again. You should make sure you are re-running your training in the normal conditions, the same as you would be using your device. You must not place your voice right next to the microphone when performing the training as you will never speak this way subsequently. You should perform your training at the same distance as you generally speak with Alexa.

If you turn of any background noise it may also help the Dot to pick up your voice specifically. You should know if you have done the voice training correctly on one Alexa device, all other devices will work better as well.

Once you have started your voice training the ring around your Amazon Echo will illuminate and you will need to read through 25 sentences. If you have said something wrong or not clear you can repeat your sentence before clicking **Next**.

After completing the voice training you have the option to complete the training again to further tune your results.

Issues with Alexa Discovering Your Smart Home Device

If while discovering your Smart Home device you are having some issues with your Echo in this chapter you will get to know how to troubleshoot the connection.

One of the first things that you should do is to make sure that your new home device is compatible with your Echo. You can find a supported list of devices at https://www.amazon.com/alexasmarthome. If your device is included on the list of supported items then you should double check to determine if a "skill" is needed to enable it to work with Alexa. There are two brands which do not need "skills" to be able to work with the Echo. They are WeMo and Phillips.

Here are the instructions you should follow to properly troubleshoot your device.

- First, you should download the companion application for your smart home device and pass the standalone setup.
- Then make sure that your device is currently connected to the same Wi-Fi network as your Amazon Echo.

- If you still have the same issue with your connection you should try restarting both devices.
- Then you should confirm that any software updates which are necessary for the home device have been performed.
- Then try to disable the skill associated with your home device and re-enable.
- You can also try discovering your devices again. You should just say to Alexa "Discover my devices" to place the Amazon Echo in discoverable mode.

Echo is Not Responding or Does Not Turn On

If your Echo is not responding or not turning on you can try a lot of ways to make your device responsive again. You should follow the next steps:

- One of the easiest ways to troubleshoot this issue is to make sure that you are using the power adapter that comes with your devices. If you use the cellular device chargers or other low level power adapters you should know that they do not provide the needed power for the Echo to operate properly.
- You should use the action button to see if Alexa will respond. After pushing the button, attempt to speak your command to Alexa again.

- When you are speaking to Alexa you should speak is clear and natural. Also, there must be no background noise.
- You should also make sure that your external speaker is at least 3 feet away from the Echo and it does not interfere with sound quality. It must be at least 8 inches from a wall or various other objects.

In most cases when the Echo refuses to listen to voice commands you can solve this by unplugging then re-plugging the device back in again. Sometimes it happens due to a software update, or because the Internet connection was interrupted. Normally the Echo operates by sending a question or phrase spoken to it to Amazon's servers, which interpret the command and tell it how to respond. In some cases, restarting the Echo may not help it. Alternatively, you can try to leave it unplugged for a few hours and then plug it back in. Some users have reported that it solved the issue. It may also happen because of another unrelated issue, like software updates or issues communicating with the Amazon servers. If Echo still does not work properly or at all, you should refer to the previous section that describes how to perform a factory reset. You will have to be set up again on an Amazon account and Wi-Fi network if you reset. In most cases, it may fix the problem. If nothing else is working you should contact Amazon's customer support through their website. The customer service team can assist with a repair or replacement if you have already tried resetting and restarting Echo.

Bluetooth Connectivity Issues with Your Echo

If your Echo Dot is having some issues while connecting to Bluetooth you should follow these steps to overcome it:

Interference: If Bluetooth is not functioning as it is supposed you should try moving your device away from anything that could potentially influence the connection. The possible interferences may be baby monitors, microwaves, or other wireless devices.

- **Battery Life**: One of the reasons of bad Bluetooth connection is the battery life of your device. If you cannot remove your battery, make sure that it is full charged. If the batteries of your device are removable and/or rechargeable you should replace or recharge the batteries.

- **Clear All Bluetooth Devices:** The other way to rectify connectivity issues is to clear and reconnect the Bluetooth device. You should navigate to *Settings* from the left navigation panel to clear your Bluetooth device. Then you should select your Alexa Device in the Settings and select *Bluetooth* > *Clear*.

Pair a New Bluetooth Device: You can also clear all devices and reconnect a new one which is the best way to test a Bluetooth device. You should select your Alexa device and then select *Bluetooth* > *Pair a New Device*. When your device enters pairing mode, you should select the device from your cellular device. You will know if your device is connected successfully when Alexa notifies you.

Streaming Issues with the Echo Dot

Normally your Wi-Fi connection may determine the streaming issues with your Echo. You can fix these issues following the next steps:

- **Reduce Wi-Fi Congestion**: You should reduce Wi-Fi congestion simply by turning off devices that you do not use to free bandwidth on your network. If your device is placed close to the ground or on the floor you should raise the device higher and move it away from any walls as they may be blocking the signal. If it does not solve the problem you should move your device closer to the router/modem.

- **Reset Your Device**: You should also restart your Echo as well as the modem to fix streaming issues. You can simply press and hold down the Microphone and Volume Down buttons at the same time. You should hold it until the light ring on your device turns orange. When the process is completed the light ring should turn blue then turn on and off again. Then navigate to your Alexa application and set up your Wi-Fi again.
- **Restart Your Device**: You can also restart your Amazon Echo by unplugging the power adapter from the wall or from the back of the device. Then you should wait a few seconds and plug your device back in.
- **Restart Your Network Device**: If you are still having issues with network connectivity of your device

you should try resetting your router or modem. It is easy to do by unplugging the network device or pressing the pin hole on the back of the network device. When you have completely rebooted your device, you should give your Echo time to connect and retry your original action.

- **Contact Your Internet Service Provider**: If all the recommendations do not help to solve the issue you should contact your Internet Service Provider for more help troubleshooting your network connection.

Bluetooth Connectivity Issues with Your Echo Dot and the Alexa Voice Remote

If you have connected your Echo with your Alexa Voice Remote but it does not work properly, you can fix it with the help of the following solutions.

- **New Batteries**: First, check the batteries as they may have lost charge. If it is so, then insert the new AAA batteries in the correct orientations into your Alexa Voice Remote.
- **Pair Remote Again**: If you have noticed that your device is not working properly with your Echo you should go into Alexa Echo settings and select the device which your remote is paired and then select *Forget Remote*.
  When you have done this, you should run through the device setup again with Echo and the Alexa Voice Remote.

Restart Your Echo Dot: If none of the options have helped you to fix this issue you should restart your device. You should simply unplug the power adapter from your device and then plug it back in.

Commonly Asked Questions

Why do I no longer hear Alexa respond when I give her a command?
Recently Amazon introduced a new feature called, Brief Mode, which shortens the amount of time you will hear Alexa's voice. Instead of hearing her say "OK", she will provide a series of beeps. To toggle this feature on or off you can simply say, "Alexa, turn off Brief Mode" or select "Alexa Voice Responses" from the settings area of the Alexa application.

Where can I find a portable battery for my Echo Plus (2nd Generation)?
Being that the second generation Echo Plus is still new there are minimal options for the device, however they do exist. The Mission Battery base can be found on Amazon.com and is compatible with the 2nd generation Echo Plus.

What do I do if I do not have a smartphone and would like to set up my Amazon Echo & smart home devices? If you do not have a smart phone or for some reason are unable to user your smart phone for setup, the Alexa application can be accessed online via the Alexa.Amazon.com. This will provide the same functionality that you would receive through your mobile device. Here you can also add Home devices and search for their corresponding skills.

How do I get started using the Alexa API to develop my own skills?

Developer.Amazon.Com provides detailed information and examples on using the Smart Home API as well as providing an Alexa Skills Kit.

How do I reset my device?

You will need a paperclip to reset the Echo. Follow these steps: turn the Echo upside down and insert the paperclip into the small hole that is labeled as RESET and press the reset button. Then hold the button for 10–20 seconds. You will see that the light ring will turn on, turn off and then turn on again before beginning the setup of Echo like when it was first received.

Conclusion

The Amazon Echo is a device that has proven to be easy to use, versatile and constantly improving with time. It is ready to use almost instantly upon removal from the box and even without the integration of third party devices and applications it is a helpful item to have in any home.

No matter if you are streaming music, reading eBooks, or simply dropping in on friends and family, this device has something for everyone. Even if there is something missing, you can bet that it won't be missing for long.

With Alexa at its core your device continuously gets the latest updates from Amazon no matter what version or generation device you may have. Your device can fit in almost any environment and there is a device for every price point.

I hope that this book has proven to be a help in not only setting up your device, but in realizing that there is more to your Echo device than you originally thought.

Thanks for reading. I hope you enjoy it. I ask you to leave your honest feedback.

I think next books will also be interesting for you:

Amazon Echo Show

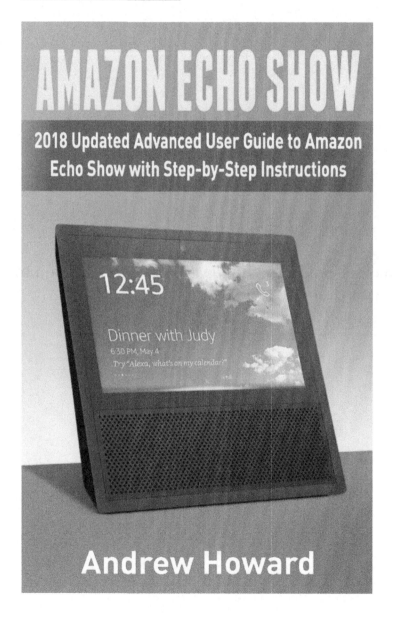

Alexa

Amazon Echo

Amazon Echo Dot

AMAZON ECHO DOT

The Ultimate User Guide to
Amazon Echo Dot
2nd Generation for Beginners

Andrew Howard

Kindle Fire HD

Amazon Echo Guide

Amazon Echo

Made in the USA
Coppell, TX
03 May 2024

32008097R00059